DISTURBING MEMORIES
& FEELINGS

LUCIANO R. CORDERO

All rights reserved. No part of this work may be reproduced, stored in a retrieval system, or transmitted, in any form or by any means, electronic, mechanical, photocopying, recording, or otherwise, without prior permission in writing from the copyright holders. The infringement of such rights may constitute an intellectual property offense.

The content of this work is the responsibility of the author and does not necessarily reflect the views of the publisher.

Published by Ibukku
www.ibukku.com
Graphic design: Índigo Estudio Gráfico
Cover design: Ronnie F. Guzmán
Copyright © 2020 Luciano R. Cordero
ISBN Paperback: 978-1-64086-735-2
ISBN eBook: 978-1-64086-736-9

Table of Contents

Aknowledgement	7
Preface	9
Introduction	13
Occultism, First Generation	17
Occultism, Second Generation	23
Occultism, Third Generation	45
My Father's Calvary	59
Horrific Encounter in a Dark Forest	67
Occultism, Other People	71
The Bright Star of the Family	77
The Effects of Occultism and Personal Growth (the author)	81
Conclusion	89
Author's Personal Comments About the Book	91
Glosary	95

Luciano. R. Cordero

He was born in la Romana, the Dominican Republic, on December 13, 1952, where he completed his elementary education. He then emigrated to Puerto Rico at the age of 20, where he lived for about a year before moving out to the United States of America, where he has been residing for the last 47 years. He also started High school in la Romana, the Dominican Republic but finished it in Manhattan, New York, where he obtained his G.E.D. Diploma. Higher education: He then attended Eugenio Maria De Hostos College, Bronx, New York, where he graduated in 1979 with a Liberal Arts. He also attended Herbert H. Lehman College, Bronx, New York, where he graduated in 1985 with a B.A. Degree in Sociology and Social Works.

Since the year 1979 until the year 2016, Luciano R. Cordero developed an extensive and successful professional career: Counselor for the City of New York, Division of Social Services, ²Welfare². Manager and Coordinator of housing assistance program for Housing Preservation & Development (H.P.D), in Bronx, New York. Coordinator and Counselor of day care services for children, 4-C in Orlando, FL. Social worker and Coordinator of social services for families and individuals for Orange County Government, Orlando, FL. Social worker and coordinator of medicals and social services with Shepherd's Hope, Inc. in Orlando, Orange County, FL. Social Worker and Coordinator of housing and social services with Osceola County Government, FL. Social worker and Coordinator of elder care services with American Eldercare in Orange county, FL. Social worker and Coordinator of housing services "Section 8" with Orange County Government, in Orlando, FL.

Luciano R. Cordero has been retired from the professional activities indicated above for the last 4 years. However, he continues to be very active as a Certified Real Estate Broker and as a Certified Notary Public for the state of Florida, professional activities which he also performed simultaneously with his other obligations named above. In the year 1997, Luciano R. Cordero relocated from New York to Kissimmee, FL. where he has been residing since then with his wife, Maria Morel, (Mery, as all people, lovingly called her).

Aknowledgement

My deep appreciation to Dr. Jose Matamoros, pastor of the Christian church, Casa Del Rey. His suggestions and advices during the early process of writing this book were of invaluable help to me. It is an honor for me to call him my friend. I also dedicate this book to my lovely wife, Maria Morel, Mery, for her patience and support, during the entire process of writing this book. In addition, I would like to thank Ronie F. Guzman for creating and designing the front and back cover of this book.

Preface

This my first book, Disturbing Memories And Feelings, was born out the need I have had for many years of telling and sharing with the reader my own real experiences of fears and terror that I lived and suffered first- hand, since my childhood until my adolescence years, as a result of the horrifying practice of witchcraft, sorcery and spiritualism carried out in my presence, by some members of my own family and by other people in the community where we all lived. These experiences were so traumatic, so frightening and so stormy for me that although these events occurred more than five decades ago, they are still alive, fresh and gravitating in my mind as if they happened in recent time, and what also became a well kept and guarded family's secret, due to the diabolic and shameful nature of this practice and because it created both in me, as well as in some members of my family, a great feeling of shame and guilt. Reasons why, more than fifty years later, I decided to write and reveal these harrowing experiences and this family's secret in this book, as a therapy and as an exorcism, for in some way free myself from those troubling memories, emotions and feelings.

This may not be the best book ever written, published or executed, but one thing that I can assure the reader is that this is an authentic, faithful, and real book based on real people and on real events and acts of occultism, which are presented to you in this book exactly as they occurred, and as I lived, saw and felt them at the time when they took place. Also, in this book, there are not ornaments, fillings, or alterations in any way, shape, or form, and I only changed the names of the members of my family who participated in these events, due to an agreement made between them and I to protect their identities and privacies. Therefore, I hope with humility that when the reader reads this book, he or she will be able to learn or to find something of importance on it. Similarly, I wish that this book will be also read by those members of my family who are still alive and who have been carrying with them the feelings of shame and guilt for all of these years so that they can also get rid of those disturbing memories emotions and feelings, the same way that the writing of this book has done for me.

All the information used in this book were obtained the following ways: using my own memories of acts, events and real manifestations of occultism executed in my presence by some members of my family and other people; utilizing stories, anecdotes and testimonies told by my own mother who participated in the practice of occultism; via stories, anecdotes and testimonies told by other members of my family such as uncles and aunts, who although they never practiced nor participated in the occult, they did witnessed its; by making use of the study of the Bible which help me to understand and recognize the tactics and strategies that Satan and his demons use to deceive, to confuse and to trap people. The study of the Bible also served me as a spiritual guide and assisted me in choosing and selecting all the biblical versicles and passages I used in this book. Similarly, I read the book: *El Gran Conflicto* of Elena G. White, which helped me to understand the spiritual battle that has been going on between good and evil almost since the beginning of humanity.

Introduction

The stories, experiences, and anecdotes told in in this book occurred between the decades of the years 50 and 70, in la Romana, a rural and small coastal community located in the southeast side of the Dominican Republic, bathed by the waters of the Caribbean Sea in the south and by the Atlantic Ocean in the North of the island. The majority of people in this place and time were superstitious. They believed in the occult and in supernatural phenomenon and forces. It was common to see people performing and engaging in activities related to witchcrafts, sorceries and spiritualism. In this community, some shamans and healers prepared incantations and infusions with natural herbs, plants and magic to treat illness, to protect people from bad spirits and to attract the good ones, or to protect them from hexes, spells, or incantations, but some shamans and healers prepared hexes, spells and incantations to harm people. It was also common to see entire families or group of friends gathering inside the houses or sitting in the backyards at night in the dark telling stories and anecdotes of sorceries, witchcrafts, and spiritualism, of witches flying on broomsticks during the night searching for children in the neighborhood to suck up their bloods and fatty fluids out o their bodies to do black magic and sorceries. They also told stories of "Zombies", dead people who had been brought back to life and controlled by someone, and of "Baca", a malignant spirit that goes around protecting the belongings of its owner under the appearance of an animal. All of these stories and narratives told in this community aroused terrors and panic in many people, including children. Many of us were afraid to walk alone in the night and in the dark. Every time some of us heard and unfamiliar or uncommon sounds or howls in the night, we associated them with "Baca", demons or diabolical and possessed dangerous wild beasts that were wandering around in the dark to harm people.

These beliefs and practices were perceived and accepted as normal behaviors and as a way of life for most people in the community. Those habits and customs were taught and passed on to many families from generation to generation. And it was in this environment and in this community where my family was born and raised, and where I was born and lived from childhood until my adolescence years. It was also in this place and in this same habitat where some members of my family and other people conducted and practiced in my presence the horrible acts of witchcrafts, sorceries, and spiritualism that marked and affected my life and the lives of all the people who directly or indirectly participated in these events. However, it is not the objective of this book to explain the history of the occult, nor it is the intention of the author to write about the struggle that has existed between good and evil since almost the beginning of humanity because this topic has already been discussed and written about by other authors and writers in religious and secular books. The purpose of this book is to reveal and to recount how the worship and the practice of occultism started in my family and how these knowledge and beliefs were taught and transmitted to my mother and her younger brother by their own father and mother; how my mother, in turn, taught and transmitted these knowledge and beliefs to some of her older daughters; and how these practices and beliefs affected and marked the lives of all the people who directly or indirectly participated in these events. Lastly, this book explains how and why some of these people broke away from these practices and managed to escape from the grasps of Satan and his demons, while others could not do it.

Occultism, First Generation

The practice of the occult in our family started with my maternal grandfather Luigi and my grandmother Mema. I never got to know my grandfather personally because he died the same year I was born, and the things I know about him, I learned it from my mother and testimonies and anecdotes told by other family members. However, I did get to know my grandmother Mema during my childhood until twelve when she passed away. My grandparents got to know each other and married when they were both adolescents and ended up having seven children, four males and three females, including my mother Yaya, one of their oldest daughters. My grandfather Luigi was a farmer, a very quiet and short man with dark skin, and a strange and mysterious look on his face. He never went to school and did not know how to read or write, but he became one of the richest and most important and influential men in the community where he lived. He was the owner of many lands; he was also a carpenter and a builder, and owned many houses that he built by himself, and he had a lot of cows, horses, chickens, and many other animals. My grandfather Luigi was also the "Wizard" and "Shaman" of the community. This person was believed to have magic and supernatural powers with the ability to communicate with spirits of the dead and control the forces of nature and the will of people. It was also believed that by only looking up to the sky and to the stars, he could predict and forecast natural events which would occur in the future, such as the weather, rain, hurricanes, earthquakes, droughts etc. Moreover, he had vast knowledge of natural and medicinal herbs and plants, and he prepared incantations to treat illness and to attract good spirits to protect some people, but he also did spells, sorceries and hexes to attract bad and malign spirits to harm someone. Furthermore, it was believed that my grandfather had the power of transforming himself in another person, in an animal, in a tree or in any other object to avoid being noticed or detected by an enemy, or by someone who might be searching for him. My grandfather was as well a womanizer who had other women beside my grandmother, whom he supported financially, and with whom he spent a lot of his money. Likewise, he was an addicted and compulsive gambler in games of chance, and before he died, he lost all of his wealth and fortune, and when he died, he left my grandmother and all of his children in poverty.

My grandmother Mema, on the other hand, was also a farmer who spent most of her time growing and taking care of vegetables and fruits in the field for the consumption of the family and she, as my grandfather Luigi, never went to school and did not know how to read or write, and as my grandfather, she also practiced the occult. My grandmother was a woman of fair complexion and fine features, but something strange and mysterious was about her. She was very skinny, old, and quiet woman who never smiled or showed affection or love to anyone. She also had big light brown-colored eyes with a penetrating and meant look on her face, and every time I look at her, I had the impression that she was always searching and examining me as if she was trying to find out what I was thinking or feeling. Her hair also attracted my attention; she had dark long, and loose hair down to her hip with white hair standing out in both sides of her temple, and every time I looked at her, I had the feeling of being in the presence of a strange, mysterious and supernatural being, a sort of a witch which always horrified me.

After the death of my grandfather Luigi, one of his older sons, Guilbert took My grandmother to live with him and built her a small wooden and dark room in the backyard of his house where she spent most of her time sitting in a wooden rocking chair looking out through a small window of that room. I remember that the distance between the room where she lived and the house where I lived with my mother and the rest of the family was of approximately three or four miles, and every time that my mother asked me to visit my grandmother or to bring her some foods, clothes or anything else, I always refused to go, but my mother forced me to do it, and I had to go against my will. I never dared to tell my mother why I never wanted to visit my grandmother in that room. She always thought that my refusal to visit her was because I did not want to walk the long distance that separated our house to my grandmother's room.

However, the real reason why I never wanted to visit my grandmother in that room was due to the fact that her physical appearance and presence in that small and dark room always made feel a lot of fear, anguish and anxiety.

Years later, my grandmother Mema died and as soon as she passed away, uncle Guilbert in a hurry, and without holding a wake, buried her body and suspiciously dismantled her room and burned all the woods. His actions intrigued and aroused suspicions in a lot of people, including his family and friends. Still, when someone asked him why he acted with such an urgency, he always said that the reason why he acted with such an urgency, he always said that he acted that way was because my grandmother suffered from pulmonary tuberculosis. Thus, he wanted to prevent members of his family and other people from moving in that room and be infected by the disease. His answer never convinced anybody, and the majority of people in the community always believed that the real reason why he buried the body of my grandmother and destroyed and burned the room with such rush was that uncle Guilbert knew that after my grandmother died, the malign demons that always lived with her stayed in her room. Hence, uncle Guilbert thought that by dismantling and burning the room, he also got rid of those demons, but the truth of what happened and of what motivated him to act the way he did only God knows since my uncle died years ago and he took that secret to his grave. However, we know for sure that my grandmother, as well as my grandfather, practiced witchcraft, sorcery and spiritualism, they with their actions and beliefs, attracted and invited Satan and his demons to their lives and to their environments. Therefore, it should not surprise anybody if these demons stayed and inhabited my grandmother's room after her dead and this, in turn, made uncle Guilbert to act the way he did.

I never found out if at any time of their lives my grandfathers knew or understood how diabolic and dangerous the practice of the occult really was, or if they were ever aware of the sin they committed with this practice, but since the majority of the people in the community where they lived saw this kind of practice as an acceptable and normal behavior, it is logical to think that my grandfathers also saw it the same way. However, whether they knew it or not, my grandfathers, with their actions, invited Satan and his demons to control their lives, their environments and sealed a pact of spiritual death with them. But even worst, my grandfathers also taught and transmitted these knowledge and beliefs to my mother and one of their sons, and my mother, in turn, passed on this knowledge and beliefs to some of her daughters. By doing, my grandfathers also invited Satan and his demons to control their offspring's lives and environment for generations. What a sad and controversial lives that of my grandfathers lived ! As the Holy Scripture says in Deuteronomy 5:9 says: « You shall not bow down to them or serve them; for I the LORD your God am a jealous God, visiting the iniquity of the fathers on the children to the third and fourth generation of those who hate me.

Occultism, Second Generation

As mentioned in the previous chapter, my maternal grandfathers not only practiced the occult themselves. They also taught and passed on this knowledge and beliefs to one of their older daughter, Yaya (my mother), and to their younger son, Memito. My mother was a fair- skinned woman, slightly heavy, built with short and dark hair. She had also big light brown- colored eyes similar to my grandmother's eyes, but unlike my grandmother, my mother was a very caring, lovely, and pleasant woman with a good sense of humor. She had the ability to laugh loudly and for a long period of time when she was telling her own jokes or when she heard somebody else telling funny stories and jokes. My mother only completed the second grade of elementary school, but she learned how to read and write very well. She read the Bible a lot, and acquired some Biblical knowledge, for which she became the community's prayer. My mother also gave birth a total of eighteen children, but five of them died in their infancies, and thirteen of us survived, seven males, and six females. We were a poor and an extended family, but my parents worked very hard to ensure that we had foods in the table and a place to live. The house where we all lived was also very small; there were only two bedrooms, one living room, one bathroom, a small brick built uncovered, and an opened porch where we all seated to get some fresh and clean air talk. In this small house there used to live a lot of people, my parents, me, some of my youngest brothers and sisters, grandchildren of my parents, and other people who came as visitors, but later they ended up living and staying permanently in the house with all of us and became part of our family. But despite our poverty and despite of so many people living in this small house, my mother always found ways to ensure that there were foods and a place to stay for all of us. I remember that my mother used the backyard of the house to plant and grow different kinds of vegetables, grains and fruit trees for the family's consumption. Since I was a child, I heard my mother all the time saying: "There's always is room for one or more, where there is room for two, there is room for three, where there is room for three, there is room for four, and so on." I also remember that when someone came to visit our community and that person did not have food to eat or a place to stay, the people of the community would tell that person to go to my mother's house because they knew that my mother would always welcome that individual in our house with open arms and she would provide him or her food and a place to stay. However, when I was twelve years old, my father passed away, and since he was the main provider in the house, we as a family suffered a great hardships to the extent of not having enough food to eat, and my mother struggled to be able to support the house and to provide for all of us. Hence, my mother decided to leave her youngest children, including me, in the care of one of my oldest sister, Brina, and traveled to Puerto Rico to search for a better future for herself and the family. Once in Puerto Rico, my mother got a job as a cook in a restaurant where she worked very hard and earned enough money to provide for all of us in the Dominican Republic. Years later, she also brought all of her children, including me to live with her in Puerto Rico, where we had the opportunity to go to school, to study, and to find work, which lifted the family out of the poverty that we all experienced in the Dominican Republic. It changed the lives and the future for the better of everyone in our family.

This was the personality and behavior of my mother that I always loved, admired and respected. However, my mother also had that other personality and behavior associated with the practice of witchcraft, sorcery, and spiritualism that I always hated and rejected because it caused me a great deal of fear, terror, and emotional and psychological pain and suffering. My mother, as my maternal grandfathers, also practiced the occult, and she served as the "Shamaness or Curandera" for the people in the community where we lived. Since I was a child, I could see people coming to our house to "Consult" with my mother to ask her for potions of natural and medicinal plants and herbs to treat their illness or the illness of their loved ones or to ask for incantations, or spells to attract the good spirits and to protect them from the bad ones, or to ask her to guess for them the winning numbers of the lottery before the drawing, for them to buy those lottery tickets numbers hoping to win the lottery and some money. But other people went to see my mother to ask her to prepare hexes and sortileges to harm other people or to protect them from sortileges or hexes done by other sorcerers or witches, or to ask her to serve as a medium to communicate with some members of their family who had died.

My mother was also the community's prayer. As such, she was often invited by some of the people in the community to pray for their loved ones in their houses, wakes, cemeteries and some other places, and many times while she was praying in some of these places, the demons possessed her in front of other people who were gathered there and she had to stop praying and ran out of those places like a bat out of hell, chased by those demons which brought her to our house, without my mother even knowing how or when she got home. Similarly, my mother was often invited by "Santeros and Santeras", or priest healers to go to pray to some dark and scary places where they invoked, venerated, and worshiped ugly and strange dark saints and figures. One night, when I was only ten years old, my mother took me with her to one of these dark places. It was a dark, long, wide, and dusty dirt floor patio, and in the exact center of it, there were several altars full of lighted candles with a lot of saints, figures, and pictures with ugly faces, and infernal and demoniacal looks. There were also a long and wide wooden table full of food, fruits and drinks, which were offered to those supernatural beings, and the spirits of these deities, in turn, manifested and possessed some of the men and women who were participating in these rites and cults. Some of these people were playing drums and tambourines, which produced a quick and ill-fated sound, they were also singing in a very strange and unknown language. But others possessed by the spirit of these supernatural beings and with widely red and scary eyes, started dancing in the dirt and dusty floor like wild animals, sweating, stinking, jumping, turning, and twisting their bodies around with quick, agile, and strong movements, following the rhythms and sounds of those drums and tambourines, raising a lot of dust out of the dirt floor with their steps and movements. Then, some of them fell to the dirt floor and started stamping, kicking in the ground, moving their scary and red eyes side to side and up and down with a cynical, sinister and mocking looks in their faces. They also started dragging, sliding and twisting their bodies and heads in the floor like snakes and like dangerous and wild beasts, staring and looking up at some of the people around them with aggressive and menacing looks in their faces, looking like they were ready to attack and harm someone. Suddenly, an infernal and demonic scream and howl came out of these people's throats, and they started talking at the same time with rasping and deep voices and in strange and unknown different languages, which appeared to come from the afterlife or from hell. I was terrified in the middle of all of this observing this madness, and as I looked around, I saw my mother running back and forth in that dark and dusty patio with a rosary and a Bible in each hand, talking to these spirits and demons and praying to those people who were possessed by these demons.

On each side of that dark patio, some people were standing underneath of some tall and dark trees. Since the reflection of lights coming from those lighted candles that were on top of those wooden tables in the center of that place were illuminating their faces, I could see that some of them appeared to enjoy and to have fun observing this infernal and collective madness stage. Still, some other people like me showed in their faces and in their looks fears, horror, panic and terror. Also, the reflection of that lights in the faces and bodies: of the people who were possessed, dancing, jumping and moving around, of those who were standing underneath those tall and dark trees, and of those horrible and ugly pictures of saints and figures in the altars, made all of us look like infernal ghosts, shadows and silhouettes, a demoniacal scenes and stage so unreal, so scary and so traumatic that I was in shock and I felt that I was in a real diabolic and infernal hell. And although I was only watching this event for only twenty or twenty five minutes, I felt that I was standing in that patio for hours. I was so terrified by this supernatural and surreal experience that I felt that my heart stopped for a while and that I was short of breath. Without telling or looking for my mother, I got out of that dark and sinister dark place running so fast that when I reached my house I was tired, sweaty and so traumatized by this experience that I did not tell anybody about it, until I wrote this book more than fifty years later.

I also remember a few times that while I was sleeping with my mother in the same room, I woke up startled and confused in the nights to see my mother possessed by bad demons and spirits, standing in front of a mirror cabinet with a cynical, infernal and hard look on her face. My mother also laughed out loud with an ironic smiles on her face, and as if she was a man, she gestured, grabbed her genitals, and spoke with a hoarse and deep voice in a very strange and unknown language. Every time that I watched my mother possessed by these demons and spirits and acting like that, I was filled with fear and terror, and I started crying and talking to her, trying to make her to come out of those trances. But she never heard me nor was she ever aware of her possession and actions because those demons and spirits robbed her of her willingness and awareness, and she stayed in a trance for twenty or twenty five minutes. Every time that this happened, I jumped out of my bed, and I went to look for some other member of my family or a neighbor to assist my mother. However, when I managed to have someone to come with me, it was nothing that this person could do to help my mother or to make her to come out of these trances because those malign demons and spirits that possessed her came and left whenever they want to, but even when they left, and my mother came out of these trances, she would go back to her bed and back to sleep as if nothing happened.

I never knew if my mother ever understood how much the events and acts of the occult she performed in my presence had affected me as a child since she never discussed it with me. Normally, when children are in the presence of their mothers and look at them at their eyes, all of what children should see and feel is love tenderness and protection, but the emotional and affective connection I had with my mother at that time of my life was quiet the opposite. One day when I was seven or eight years old, I looked at my mother in her eyes, and innocently and spontaneously, I told her: "Mother, you have mean eyes like grandmother's eyes." She only looked at me and did not say a word, but several years later, when I was already an adult, my mother and I had a conversation, and she with some resentment and remorse, reminded me of those words that I told her when I was a child. Suddenly, her remark hit me and made me react and reflect, and it was at this moment when I knew how much my child's comment had hurt her, but it also made me realize how much and how deep those horrifying experiences of witchcraft, sorcery, and spiritualism that I observed and lived with her since my childhood, had marked and affected me. Because when I looked at my mother in her eyes and compared her "Mean eyes" with the "Mean eyes" of my Grandmother, Mena, all what I was doing, although I did not know it at that time, was that I was unconsciously revealing and showing all the traumas and feelings of fear, horror and terror that I lived and experienced with my mother, as a result of the acts and events of occultism that I witnessed since I was a child.

During all the times that I saw my mother possessed by those demons which always followed her, one of the thing that impacted me the most, and which always stayed registered in my mind, was seeing in her face and eyes that mean, cynical and infernal looks and smile, thus every time I looked at her in her face and eyes, even when those demons did not possess her, I thought that I still saw those same looks and smiles in her face and eyes. And which were also the same looks that I saw in my grandmother's face and eyes when she was alive, and that always terrified me every time that I went to visit her in that dark and small room where she died. However, during the conversation I had with my mother, as an adult, I looked at her in her face and eyes, and with sincere love and remorse in my heart, I told her: "Mother, please forgive me for my child's comment. I did not mean to offend or to disrespect you, I was only a child at that time and I was just saying what I honestly and innocently saw and felt at that moment." She also looked at me in my eyes with love and understanding and told me: "I know my son you were only a child when you said those words. I love you so much, and I forgive you." After this, we hugged each other, kissed and cried together for several minutes. However, later on, I started reflecting in this conversation that I had with my mother, and I also realized that she seemed not to be aware of how much her practice of witchcraft, sorcery and spiritualism in my presence really hurt me, nor she seemed to realize the sin that she was committing with the practice of the occult, since she never talked to me about it nor she ever asked me to forgive her for it. A behavior from my mother that I understood because during the time she practiced the occult, it was an accepted and normal behavior for most people. However, there were many times that I saw my mother in the house reading the Bible, praying with fervors, reciting verses aloud and singing Christian songs, which always gave me the impression that she was trying to break away from the practice of the occult, but while she was doing all of this, she was also engaging in activities and diabolic acts of witchcraft, sorcery and spiritualism. My mother wittingly or unwittingly, had invited Satan and his demons to her live, her house and her family. She worshiped these entities and deities for so many years that she created a strong bond and a strong relationship with them, to the point that her desires coincided with their desires and those demons possessed and controlled her as they wished. With her behavior and actions, my mother had also sealed a pact and a commitment with these dark and malign beings. Although she may tried to run away from them, she could not do it; it was too late for her; Satan and his demons never abandoned her; they haunted and chased my mother even after she died. But in spite of all of my mother's trails and errors, she was a woman who had great human values and virtues, and she was also the person who gave me life, raised me, and took care me, and for those reasons, I always loved, honored, respected and admired her like no other person in my life.

My mother died approximately twenty years ago, but she suffered a lot before and after her death because although the doctors who assisted her declared my mother clinically dead, and although her body had already started to decompose up to stink, there were still some beats and palpitations in the middle of her belly which could be felt and heard. And since the doctors never had seen or experienced something like that, they were surprised and alarmed with this phenomenon, reasons why they started investigating in an attempt to find a scientific or a logical explanation for this mystery. But despite of all their efforts, the doctors could not find a logical explanation for this event nor could they stop those palpitations and beats in the belly of my mother. Thus, they discharged her from the hospital, and two of my sisters brought her back home, but since my mother's body continued to decompose, and the palpitations and beats in her belly still did not disappeared, my sisters brought to the house some Christian priests and a pastors, hoping that they could assist my mother to get rid of those beats and palpitations to be able to burry her. However, the prayers and exorcisms performed by those priests and pastors did not stop those beats and palpitations and my sisters in desperation, and as a last result, solicited the service of a local shaman to assist my mother, and as soon as he examined her body, the shaman concluded that the reason for those beats and palpitations in her belly was due to a spell she had years ago to protect her from hexes and malign spirits. He also explained that this spell needed to be removed for my mother be able to die in peace; after that, the shaman performed some rites and prayers, and minutes later and as if by magic, those beats and palpitations from my mother's belly stopped and disappeared.

But at the same time, those beats and palpitations stopped, a sinister and infernal moaning, and a shriek came out of my mother's throat, followed by a strong and furious wind that was felt in that room which opened the door widely with violence. Then, this mysterious and infernal entity/energy left the room at full speed and crashed into Nenita's body, one of my mother's granddaughter, who was in the house's backyard the and who came from a nearby town to be with my mother, possessing her. As soon as Nanita felt the impact of this diabolic force, she started convulsing and trembling, and some of the male members of the family who were in the backyard had to hold Nanita to prevent her from falling in the ground and hurt herself. But Nanita also started to jump and to twist her body violently with such incredible force and strength that it was almost impossible to hold or to restrain her, but all of the sudden, she stopped trembling and convulsing, and she started talking in a very strange and mysterious language. Then she stopped talking and remained silent and still for a while, then with a cynical and mocking smile on her face, she looked at Franchi, one of my mother's grandson who was still holding her, and with a hoarsely and deep voice, as if she was a man and the demon that always possessed my mother, she ordered and said to Franchi: "Kiss my hand and ask for my blessing." Franchi scared, confused, and without knowing what to do or what to say; he looked at the other people who were standing in the backyard, as if he was asking them with his eyes what to do, then someone from the crowd shouted to him: "Just do what she is asking you to do for the demon to go away and leave Nanita alone." Franchi, still scared and trembling, kissed the hand of Nanita, and as if she was my mother, he, with babbling voice, asked Nanita for her blessing, and as soon as Franchi did this, that malign demon left Nanita's body. And as she was coming out of that trance, Franchi was still holding her, and Nanita, confused and disoriented, looked at him and said: What is happening, why are you holding me? Franchi then explained to her exactly what happened, and Nanita angry and ashamed for being part of that diabolical experience asked: Why me?, then she said: "I have never asked nor I have ever been part of something like this before" "I am living this place right now." After saying those words, Nanita picked up all of her belongings she had in the house, went to the nearest bus station, took a bus, and returned to Haina, the small town where she lived and from where she came to be with my mother at her death bed. The next day after this event, the body of my mother was finally buried.

The act of this demonic possession of the granddaughter of my mother, Nanita, and the attack of this demon on my mother's grandson, Franchi, is a clear example that Satan and his demons never settled for having possessed and tormented my maternal grandparents, my mother and some of my sisters, but they are also pretending to deceive, confuse and to entrap in their grips this new generation descendant of my maternal grandparents. Nanita was only fifteen years old and Franchi only sixteen when this happened; they were innocent adolescents who never before had experienced nor had they ever participated in any act of witchcraft, sorcery, or spiritualism. My family's maternal side is large and extended; my grandparents had seven children, including my mother, who in turn, had thirteen children, and her other brothers and sisters had their own children and so on. Hence, it was impossible for me to know them all and to be able to find out if there are or if there were other members of my family who practiced or are still practicing the occult, I really do not know that. However, I know that Satan and his demons have a lot of power to deceive, confuse and to entrap in their grips a lot of people. Thus, I will not be surprised if some other family members have been seduced and entrapped by Satan and his demons. But even if there are some other family members worshiping Satan and his demons with the practice of the occult, they are not alone because there is an army of men and women of our family who are always praying with fervor and faith, asking God for the spiritual protection of those family members and for the world as well because we know that there is a spiritual war going on between the reign of Satan and the reign of God, but at the end Satan will be defeated. 1 John 5:4 "For whatever is born of God overcomes the world; and this is the victory that has overcome the world- our faith."

I lived in New York when I received the new of my mother's death in the Dominican Republic, and her passing away hit me very hard. I was depressed for a long time, and although my brothers and sisters insisted that I should travel there to be at her funeral wake and burial, I did not go because I wanted to preserve in my mind and heart the image and the memory of my mother as when she was alive. However, when I later found out that my sisters had used the service of a sorcerer to assist her to die, that made me feel sad and guilty at the same time because if I had been there, I would have never allowed a sorcerer to assist my mother to die, and I would rather have preferred to burry her with those palpitations and beats in her belly. Because by allowing that sorcerer to assist my mother and to touch her body before she was buried, it was like asking and giving permission to Satan and his demons to once again violates, own and possess my mother's body and soul. And to allow Satan and his demons to dictate when and how she should die and be buried, a right that only belongs to God, not to them. What a pitiful existence and death that of my mother who, instead of repenting for all her sins and choose the peace, light, and tranquility which only God can offers, through his son Jesus Christ, she instead chose to worship Satan and his demons with the practice of the occult! Deuteronomy 18: 10-13 "There shall not be found among you anyone who makes his son or his daughter pass through the fire, or one who practices witchcraft, or a soothsayer, or one who interprets omens, or a sorcerer, or one who conjures spells, or a medium, or a spiritualist, or one who calls up the dead. For all who do those things are an abomination to the lord, and because of these abominations the Lord your God drives them out from before you. You shall be blameless before the Lord your God".

My uncle Memito, on the other hand, was the youngest son of my maternal grandparents and as all of their children, Memito was born and grew up in the countryside, where he worked and cultivated the land. He also worked as a bricklayer and as a carpenter, professions he learned from his father, Luigi. Memito was a very quiet, reserved, and mysterious individual. He was a short man like his father, but had strong and muscular body and arms with cracked, rough hands filled with rough calluses, as a result, maybe, of the physical activities he performed as a carpenter and as a bricklayer. Memito, like my mother, learned from my grandfather the occultism, and he also practiced it, and around him endless anecdotes and stories were woven. He learned from his father how to transform himself into another person, in an animal, in a tree, or in any other object to hide from people and avoid being detected by his enemies. I remember a long story about Memito that was always told in my house by my mother and by other members of my family, saying that in the community where Memito lived, there also lived a very rich and influential man, Emilio Fraduc, who had a son named Maximiliano, a spoiled brat and troublemaker young man who was known for raping under- aged females children and other women in the community. He was also known for physically abusing and beating up people who did not please him on his wishes or demands. For going to bars and restaurants where he ate foods, drank alcohol and left those places without paying his bills and always got away with, due to his reputation and intimidation, and although most people in the community hated Maximiliano, he was also feared by most people. Nobody dared to confront him or report his crimes and abuses to the local authorities for fear of retaliations from him or his consenting father, Emilio Fraduc, the richest and most powerful man in the community.

However, one day, my uncle, Memito, was sitting at a table in a bar, drinking alcohol accompanied by one of the women who frequently attended that place and suddenly Maximiliano showed up in that bar and sat down in a table next to the table where my uncle was sitting. He then started looking at the woman who was sitting at the table with Memito, and in a commanding tone of voice told her: "Hey, I want you to come and sit next to me in my table. You should be here with me instead of being with that poor man who has no money to buy you drinks and take care of you". Memito immediately held the woman firmly by her arm and calmly looked at Maximiliano and told him: "If you are a real man come to my table and take her with you," and Maximiliano, in a menacing and threatening manner replied to Memito: "Do you really know who am I" and Memito answered: "Sure, I know who you are, a rapist and a man who goes around abusing, hurting people and getting away with it because everybody is afraid of you, but know you are facing a real man who is not afraid of you." Maximiliano, enraged by the words of Memito, approached the table where Memito was sitting down with the woman and unleashed a punch aimed to the face of my uncle, but Memito was prepared; he dodged the punch and grabbed an empty glass bottle of beer that was on the table and hit Maximiliano with it in his head dropping him down. Maximiliano stunned and bleeding profusely from his head, tried to get up to continue fighting, but Memito this time grabbed a chair and started hitting him all over his body and head and Maximiliano bleeding and unconsciously dropped down again to the floor. Memito then left money on the table to pay his bills and quietly walked out of the bar, and although there were a lot of people in the bar watching the fight, nobody did anything to protect or to help Maximiliano during the fight with Memito. They were so surprised or may be happy to see that someone had finally dared to put Maximiliano in his place with that beating, a man who for years terrorized and abused the community. Only the bar owner dared to call the ambulance, which minutes later came to the bar, carried Maximiliano out, and brought him to the hospital. He received medical attention for his injuries and remained there for hours, laying in bed and recuperating from his beating and injuries. The police were also notified of that incident, and the new of Maximiliano's beating quickly spread out through the community like wildfire. When Emilio Fraduc, Maximiliano's father found out what had happened to his son, he was so furious and angry that he swore to kill Memito whenever he finds him. Since he was an influential and powerful man in the community, he ordered the police to look and find Memito as soon as possible dead or alive.

Emilio Fraduc knew Memito very well because he had hired my uncle to do bricklayer and carpenter works in his house and in his ranch and farm, but even though he and the police were searching and looking for Memito, and despite the fact that Memito never left the community where he lived, days and months went by, and they could never find him. Emilio Fraduc was so concerned and furious for not being able to find Memito that he offered a monetary reward to any person who could tell him or the police Memito's whereabouts that will lead to his capture, and although from time to time he received information from someone about Memito's whereabouts, when Emilio Fraduc or the police went to those places, Memito, as if by an act of magic, disappeared and they could never find him.

One afternoon, while Memito was walking in a narrow and solitary road, he saw at the distance an imposing figure of a man in a white horse carrying a gun on his side riding toward him. Memito immediately recognized that man in that horse, it was Emilio Fraduc, but without hesitation, Memito evaluated his situation: he could not walk back or use an alternate route or hide from Emilio Fraduc because he had already noticed the presence of my uncle in the area, and if Memito would had taken any of these actions, it would arose suspicion and curiosity on Emilio Fraduc. Thus, Memito, with a steady and resolute straight face, walked toward Emilio Fraduc, pulled a cigar from his pocket, and with the cigar in his hand asked him: Sir, do you by any chance have a lighter so that I can light up this cigar? Emilio Faduc looked Memito from head to toe and pulled a lighter out of his shirt pocket, gave it to Memito and said: "For some time I have been looking for a man named Memito" then he gave Memito the physical description of that man and asked him: ¿Have you by any chance seen a man that matches that description? But before Memito answered Emilio Fraduc's question, he lighted up the cigar, gave the lighter back to Mr. Fraduc, thanked him for it, and calmly and coldly said to him "I am sorry sir, but I have not seen anyone fitting that descriptions. But I can assure you that if I ever see that man, I will notify you or the police." After saying that, Memito inhaled and exhaled a huge puff of smoke from the cigar and continued walking as if nothing had happened. Emilio Fraduc never suspected that the man he had been looking to kill was standing in front of him and talking to him just minutes ago. The police nor Emilio Fraduc could ever find Memito because Memito had the ability to transform into another person, an animal, a tree or any other physical object to avoid detection and be identified by his enemies.

For many years, it was very difficult for me to believe in the story of physical transformation of Memito. However, based in some biblical knowledge I have and the fact that as child I witnessed a lot of diabolic acts and possessions in my family that at the time seemed incredible to me, now I have no doubt in my mind that this is possible and real. Because Satan and his demons themselves have the power to transform their physical appearances to be able to confuse, deceive and control people. Thus, it should not surprise anybody if the followers of Satan and his demons, such as my uncle, was also able to transform himself to hide, confuse and deceive other people. Memito's life was a real mystery, and he always gave the impression of being running away or hiding from something or from someone. He always moved around alone and never stayed in the same place for long period of time. Nobody, including his family, ever knew if he ever married or had children. He also used to disappear and distance himself from his mother and relatives for years and nobody ever knew of his whereabouts, but in any given day, he would show up at the family's house unannounced and without being expected by his family, where he would stay for a couple of days. But suddenly, he would leave the house and disappeared for years, without telling anybody of his whereabouts. Uncle Memito was a real enigma, not even his family ever got to know him well, and even to this day, nobody knows whether he is still alive or dead. (2 Co. 11:14-15) "And no wonder, for even Satan disguises himself as an angel of light. So it is no surprise if his servants, also, disguise themselves as servants of righteousness. Their end will correspond to their deeds."

Occultism, Third Generation

Marla was the first and oldest daughter of all my mother's children, and as far back as I can remember, she suffered from some kind of a mental illness problem. For this reason, Marla always lived with my mother and with the rest of the family in the house. I never knew what exactly caused Marla's mental illness, nor I ever knew for sure if my mother at any given time taught or passed on to Marla the knowledge of the occult, or if my sister ever practiced it. However, during the time I lived with Marla and my family, from my childhood through my adolescent years, I could see that Marla, at times, showed some strange behaviors. Sometimes she looked disoriented and disconnected from reality, and from all of us. She also used to go into a dark and solitary room of the house and stayed quietly and silently in a corner or under a bed for hours, and many times we had to force her to leave the room literally. Other times we could hear Marla talking to herself or talking and fighting with an imaginary being, saying and repeating these same words over and over again: "Leave me alone, do not touch me criminal donkey." However, with the exception of those mental lapses, Marla, for most part, showed great mental lucidity, she behaved and acted like any normal and ordinary person. She talked and participated in conversations with all of us, and she always understood and did what it was expected from her in the house. Marla had the ability to cook meals for herself, and for all of us, she cleaned the house, bathed and groomed herself, ironed clothes, washed ditches, washed her own clothes and the clothes of others, and did any other chores in the house without any assistance from anyone.

My mother always stated that Marla's mental problem started at a very young age, after she married a man who beat her when she was pregnant, and since that incident, according to my mother, Marla began showing her mental illness. During many years I believed and accepted my mother's explanation as to what caused Marla's mental illness, but now as an adult, and after analyzing Marla's behaviors at that time, I have doubts and suspicions, not only on what could have happened to Marla that caused her mental perturbations, but also on whether or not my mother taught and passed on to Marla the knowledge of the occult, and on whether or not Marla ever practiced the occult. These doubts and suspicions are based on the facts that even before Marla was born, my mother had already been practicing the occult. My mother also taught and passed on this knowledge to three of her youngest daughters, who were born after Marla was born. Thus, it is logical for me and for anybody else to think that since Marla was the first and the oldest daughter of my mother, very well could have been Marla the first of my mother's daughter to learn from my mother the occult, the first of my mother's daughter to practice it, and the first of my mother's daughter who was chased and possessed by demons. But even more, it may well have been that those same demons caused Marla's mental illness. Marla died around twenty- five years ago, a few years before my mother passed away, and I never asked any of them about it. Hence, only God knows what really happened to Marla. May God receive Marla's soul! Deuteronomy 18:10:10 "Let no one be found among you who sacrifices their son or daughter in the fire, who practices divination or sorcery, interprets omens, engages in witchcraft."

Diana, was the second daughter of my mother, and she also learned from my mother the practice of the occult; and as my mother, she also practiced witchcraft, sorcery, and spiritualism, and was also chased, possessed, and tormented by demons until her death. I did not spend a lot of time with Diana because she married at a very young age and lived with her spouse and her four males children in the country's capital. But from time to time, she came to visit us in the town were we lived and although, on the one hand, I was happy to see her when she came to visit us, on the other hand, her presence in the house made me feel anxious and tense because as soon as she arrived, the atmosphere in the house changed and turned heavy, filled with negative energies. Her presence in the house was like a warning or an omen that some diabolic acts of possessions or some manifestations of witchcraft, sorcery, and spiritualism was going to take place in the house, which always did occur. One morning Diana was sitting in a chair in the kitchen drinking a cup of coffee but all of a sudden, and without finish drinking the coffee, she put the cup aside in a table and with a mocking and infernal smile and look in her face, she started first moving her head very slowly from side to side and up and down. Diana then got up from the chair and started jumping so high that she almost touched the ceiling with her head; afterwards, she fell in the floor, and some infernal and macabre howling and screams came out of her throat, and she started gesturing and talking in a language that nobody understood. Then, she stopped talking and started dragging, twisting and sliding her body in the floor like a sneak. Suddenly, she got up from the floor and grabbed a huge can full of water in the kitchen table and drank so much water from that can that it was impossible for a normal person to drink. After that, Diana then sad down quietly in the chair and with and with a disoriented, distant, and lost look on her face, as if she just woke up from a dream and with a surprising look on her face, she stared at the other members of the family who were there and asked: What happened? Why is everybody looking at me? Why there is this mess in the kitchen?. These were the same questions that Diana always asked when she came out of her trance from those infernal and diabolic possessions, but, as usual, nobody ever answered her questions, because everybody in that kitchen knew that although Diana was never aware when these demons possessed her, nor she ever knew what she did or said when she was in those trances, Diana did know that these demons always controlled and possessed her and that they came and went whenever they wanted to.

Diana's husband never practiced the occult himself, but he allowed her to engage in such practice in the house where they both lived with their four children. However, years later, Diana's husband repented of his sins and committed his life to Christ, and tried for years to convince Diana to repent of her sins and follow him in his footsteps. He invited and took Diana with him to church, he studied the Bible with her and prayed and sang Christian songs in the house with her, but despite all of his efforts, Diana did not listen to him and never stopped practicing witchcraft, sorcery, and spiritualism. As years passed by, he got so tired of trying to convince Diana to repent of her sins and to stop practicing the occult that one day he took his four sons with him and left the house, leaving Diana alone. In the meantime, my sister continued worshiping Satan and those demons with the practice of the occult, but years later, old, sick and demented; Diana ended up in a Nursing Home Facility Center, where she spent the rest of her life on a bed or sitting down in one of the sofas inside of the institution talking to herself and arguing with those demons which always chased her. It was also common to see Diana sitting in a rocking chair in the balcony of the Facility Center fighting with those demons and saying and repeating over and over these same words: "Leave me alone, I told you to leave me alone. I do not want anything with you, I do not want to talk to you." After a couple of years of staying in the Facility Center, Diana died, and when her husband and her sons were notified of her dead, they went to the center, picked up her dead body and buried her. What a sad and tragic life that of my sister Diana who, by dedicating her life to worship Satan and his demons with the practice of the occult, not only surrender her soul to them but also she separated herself from the presence of God and her family, ending her life alone and helpless in a Senior Citizen Facility Center. As my maternal grandfathers, Diana, my mother, my uncle Memito and my sister Marla, never repented from her sins, never committed her life to Christ and never stopped practicing witchcraft, sorcery, and spiritualism. Hence, Satan and his demons never abandoned her, and they chased and tortured her until the last day of her life. (Leviticus 20:27) "A man or a woman who is a medium or a necromancer shall surely be put to death. They shall be stoned with stones; their blood shall be upon them."

Brina was the third daughter of my mother, and as Marla and Diana, she also learned from my mother the practice of witchcraft, sorcery, and spiritualism. From all of my sisters, Brina was the one I got along with best and the one I trusted most because although she only completed the four primary grades, she learned how to read, speak and write very well, and we could talk about many different topics. We used to spend a lot of time sitting down on a sofa or lying down in a bed, talking about ours desires, our fears and about our plans for the future. However, like my mother, Brina also had that other personality and behavior associated with the practice of witchcraft, sorcery, and spiritualism that disturbed me and which made me to distance myself from her. As my mother, Brina, practiced the occult and had knowledge of medicinal plants and herbs and she also became a "Charmaness" or "Curandera" in the community. Since I was a child, I saw a lot of people coming to the house to "Consult" with Brina and ask her for potions of medicinal plants or herbs to cure some kind of illness for them or some other family members. They also asked Brina for incantations and spells to protect them or their families from bad spirits and to attract the good ones, but some other people went to see her to ask for sorceries and hexes to cause harms to somebody else or to ask Brina to serve as a medium for them to be able to communicate with the spirits of their love ones who had died. Likewise, Brina was possessed by infernal and demoniacal entities and many times I witnessed those possessions. One afternoon I came back to the house from school and since I was hungry, I went straight to the kitchen to get something to eat, and while I was in the kitchen, I could hear the laughing and the conversations that Brina was having with other members of my family in the living room. But suddenly, there was silence, and the laughs and conversations stopped. Since I was curious for that silence, I went to the living room to find out what was going on, and it was then when I saw Brina sitting on a sofa very quietly with a mocking, cynical, infernal, and diabolic smile in her face. Suddenly, she started first moving her head very slow side to side, then she started moving her head up and down and down and up very fast and with such violence that it looked like she was going to take off her head out of her neck. Then she started making grinding teeth sounds and out of her throat came out some screeches that seemed to be coming from beyond the grave. She also started gesturing and talking like a man with a very deed and hoarsely voice. Moment later, Brina sat down again in that sofa and stayed there silently for a moment, but suddenly her hands and fingers started to transform like animal's claws and with a menacing and intimidating look on her face, she started staring at the people who were there in the living room. Then, like a wild and dangerous animal ready to attack, and with a defiant and threatening look still on her face, she got up of that sofa with an agile and feline move started gesturing and talking in an unknown language. Seconds later, she jumped so high that her head almost touched the house ceiling and fell to the floor where she remained for a while without moving and with her eyes closed. Suddenly, as if she had just woke up from a dream, she started opening her eyes slowly, and surprised and confused; she looked at all the people who were in the room an asked: Why am I lying in the floor? What has happened? But as usual, nobody said anything or answered her questions because everybody in that room understood that those demons that possessed Brina had the freedom to come and go whenever they wanted, and there was nothing that anybody could do to prevent those demons from possessing Brina. These were the same infernal entities that always possessed my mother and my other sisters.

Brina continued practicing the occult for a long time, but years later, she started showing some remorse

and repentance for this practice. There were times that she was possessed by demons and after coming out of her trances, she to looked sad and depressed, saying:
² I am sick and tired of this filthy curse, these bloody demons do not leave me alone. I have three children and I do not want them to learn from me this filthy and infernal practice that has existed in our family for generations. I have to find a way of getting out of this.
² I remember that one of my oldest brothers, William, a pastor missionary and the only Christian member of my family at that time, spent a lot of time talking to Brina, my mother, and my other sisters who practiced the occult, trying to persuade them to stop the practice of the occult and to repent of all of their sins. Many times, I also witnessed William sitting my mother and my sisters each on a chair, and with the Bible in one hand and the other hand in their heads, he prayed with faith and devotions and ordered those demons to go away and leave my mother and sisters alone. He also preached to my mother and sisters and used to tell them that the only way they could free themselves from Satan and his demons was by stopping to worship them with the practice of the occult, to repent for all of their sins, to pray with faith and devotion to God and to surrender to Christ. After some time, and maybe following the advise of William, Brina started to study the Bible and prayed with faith and devotion. She also started participating in Christian cults, singing Christian songs in the house, jointed a Christian church and stopped practicing the occult. But in spite of all of her effort to distance herself from Satan and

his demons, they never gave up chasing her, and there were moments when they attacked and tried to possess her in the same church, as well as in the house and in other public places. But thanks to Brina's perseverance and resilience, and thanks to all the help she received from her pastor and other church members, Brina was able to resist Satan's attacks and his demons, and she was finally able to free herself from them.

Brina's repentance not only saved and protected her from Satan's and his demons but it also helped Brina to protect and prevent her own children from learning the occult and following her footsteps of worshiping Satan and his demons with the practice of witchcraft, sorcery, and spiritualism. Brina's two daughters later accepted and surrendered their lives to Christ, and even today, they all attend the same Christian church and it is common to see them walking in the streets and going around house to house preaching and talking the words of God. Although, Brina's son has not yet surrendered his live to Christ, he has a great respect for the Christian faith and fear of God. But even more, Brina with her action shielded and prevented her future descendants and generations from learning the occult and from falling into the grasp of Satan and his demons. In addition, Brina was also able to stop and brake once and for all with that filthy and diabolical family's heritage of witchcraft, sorcery, and spiritualism that has been going on in our family for generations. Praise the Lord! Deuteronomy 5:9-10 "You shall not bow down to them or serve them; for I the Lord your God am a jealous God, visiting the iniquity of the fathers on the children to the third and fourth generation of those who hate me, but showing steadfast love to thousands of those who love me and keep my commandments."

Niurka was one of my mother's youngest daughters and as my other sisters, she also learned from my mother the occult. As all of them, she practiced witchcraft, sorcery, and spiritualism. Niurka used to keep an altar in a corner of one of the house's rooms filled with saints, horrible pictures, ugly faces, lighted candles, foods, and flowers offered to those entities. Of all my mother's daughters, Niurka was physically the most attractive, she was also cheerful, dynamic, studious, and friendly, full of dreams and hopes. She always wanted to finish school, find a good job, marry, have children, and a stable family, and due to her physical and personal attributes, her dreams and goals seemed to be within her reach. However, Satan and his demons seemed to have other plans for her. They attacked and chased Niurka in a different way as they had attacked and chased my mother and my other sisters. One night while everybody in the house was sleeping, her altar caught on fire, and if it had not been because one of my brother woke up on time and stopped the fire, the entire house would have been burned down together with all the people who were sleeping in it. After that incident, and for some mysterious reason, Niurka suddenly, started feeling and looking sad and depressed, she also distanced herself from friends and family members, stopped attending school, and started engaging in sexual relationships with different men, without knowing them well and without formalizing a stable relationship with any of them. As years passed by, Niurka continued living a kind of crazy and irresponsible life, and she ended up having four male children by four different fathers, and every time that these men found out that Niurka was pregnant with one of their babies, they all left her with her pregnancy, and none of them ever took care of any of these children. Thus, every time Niurka gave birth to each of her four children, she gave that child to my mother, who ended up taking care of all of Niurka's children and raised them until they all became adults, while Niurka continued living her life as if everything was normal.

Niurka's emotional and spiritual instability was so out of control that we thought that she was going to end up in a mental hospital facility, but when everything in her life seemed to go from bad to worst, Niurka met Julio, a Christian man of faith who spoke to her the words of God and invited her to his church. Afterward, Niurka started reading and studying the Bible with Julio. She also stopped practicing the occult, repented for all of her sins, and a year later, she got to marry Julio, the good man that she always dreamed of, and who showed her the way to Christ and helped her to escape from the grasps of Satan and his demons. But even more important, Niurka established a new and good relationship with all four of her children, and with time, she gained the respect and admiration from all of them. They all forgave her for not caring and raising them. Besides, two of her sons surrendered their lives to Christ and jointed her in the same church where she attended. Niurka and her husband, Julio lived together a very happy life for more than forty years, preaching together the words of God, until my sister died two years ago, at the age of seventy- two. I was at my sister's side at the hospital, where she was lying down in a bed, a day before her death. She could not talk, but I had the feeling that she listened to me when I talked to her. I also grabbed and held both of her hands, and I could see reflected in her face such serenity, tranquility, and peace that can only be seen and observed in those people whose souls before dying are at peace with God, with themselves, and with their peers. Colossians 1:12-13 "And giving joyful thanks to the father, who has qualified you to share in the inheritance of his holy people in the kingdom of light. For he has rescued us from the dominion of darkness and brought us into the kingdom of the Son he loves."

My Father's Calvary

My father was a tall, thin, athletic, and dark skinned individual who was born in the country side. He never attended school, the little he knew of reading and writing, he learned it from my mother. However, my father was a responsible hard working man, and he was able to get a job in one of the most important sugar mill in the country at that time, the Gulf And Western of La Romana, the Dominican Republic. His job consisted in conducting and operating the locomotive and the ironed wagons where he transported the sugar canes from the sugarcane plantations to the sugar mill and the refineries, where the sugar canes were processed and converted into sugar. This was a hard and demanding job with no regular hours, schedules or shifts. This job required from the workers to be ready and available to work when called at any time days or nights, under any weather conditions, consequently, my father spent most of his time at work and out of the house. I did not get to know my father well because he died when I was only twelve, but I observed his conduct and behaviors during the time I lived in the house with him, My father used to drink almost every days until he got drunk; he also smoked two or three pack of cigarettes daily, but despite this, he never missed a day of work, nor he ever showed any indication of being sick. Thus, my father's addictions to alcohol and cigarettes was never a concern for any of us in the family because, at that time, most people in the community, including my family, did not have any knowledge of the harmful and negative effects that drinking alcohol and smoking cigarettes had on people's health. Also, we did not understand that alcoholism was a disease, we all had the wrong idea that an alcoholic person was someone who did not work, someone who was ragged or dirty, walking drunk in the street, doing his or her physiological needs in the streets and in other public places, or a drunk person sleeping in the streets and in any other public places. Since my father never showed that type of behaviors, we saw his addictions as something normal, but in reality my father was a very sick individual, addicted to alcohol and cigarettes. I often saw my father coming to the house drunk late at nights or early mornings, but minutes after he went to bed, a messenger from the sugar mill would come to the house riding a bicycle to inform him that he had to report to his work right away. But my father, sleepy, tired and drunk made great efforts to get up from his bed to dress up and go to work, but since he could not do it by himself, my mother had to assist him in dressing up and placing in his shoulder, a heavy ironed, black gaslight full of gas that was one of the tools my father used to do his job. My mother also had to hold my father and almost carry him out of the house for the fresh air to wake him up before he could start walking toward the place where he worked. Since my father did not any mean of transportation, he had to walk three or four miles to be able to reach his place of work. I was just a child when all of this was taking place. I could not understand why my father behaved in such manner or why he had to go to work in such terrible bad shape. Every time I witnessed this, it made me feel very sad, and with tears in my eyes, I got out of bed, walked out of the house in the street, watching my father, drunk, tired and sleepy, walking like a zombie along that, lengthy, solitary and dark street. My father also wobbled as he walked, due to that big, black and heavy ironed gaslight which was hanging in one of his shoulder. I remember staying in that street watching him until he disappeared in the distance, and in the darkness of that long street, until I could no longer see him.

During the time I lived with my father, I also noticed changes in his behavior and personality that worried and confused me as a child. When my father was sober and not drinking in the house, he seemed to be shy, distant, sad, and depressed. He often sat quietly and alone in a chair in the house's balcony or outside under a tree in the back yard. Although my father was the main provider in the house, he never had an opinion or a saying, and never made decisions about anything in the house. His presence was almost never felt, and the only time he spoke o say anything to any of us was when he wanted someone to go to the store for him to buy a bottle of rum or a pack of cigarettes. However, when my father drank alcohol and got drunk, his personality and behavior completely changed, he seemed to be the happiest man in the world, he talked all the time, sang songs, and laughed all the time. He also danced, told jokes, anecdotes, and he even sat some of his little children, including me, on his laps hugging and playing with us. As a child, I did not understand my father's mood swing, behavior, and change of personality which always intrigued me. Since I did not have an explanation for his conduct and behaviors, I always asked myself the following questions: What's wrong with my father? Why does he have to drink alcohol and get drunk almost every day? Why does he have to go to work drunk? Why does he behave one way when he is drunk and another way when he is not drunk? But although, as a child, I asked myself all of these questions, I never got the answers to these questions because I never dared to asked them to my father, my mother or to any other family's members. However, years later, as an adult, I asked those same questions first to my mother, who said that she could not answer my questions because according to her, my father was a very quiet and private man, and he rarely talked to her about his feelings and emotions. Then, I asked these same questions to uncle Trino, one of my mother's oldest brothers who was a good friend of my father since they were both children, and who also knew very well the type of relationship that my parents had even before they got married. Uncle Trino stated that before my father married my mother, he was always a very friendly and likeable young man who never drank alcohol or smoke cigarettes, but about a year later, after they got married, my father started to look sad and started drinking alcohol, and smoking cigarettes. Uncle

Trino also believed that the reason for such changes in my father's personality and habits was due to the fact that although my father always knew that my mother practiced witchcraft, sorcery, and spiritualism, he never believed in the occult. Thus, he often asked my mother to stop this practice, but she never listened to my father's request. She continued practicing the occult, and this, according to uncle Trino, created a lot of frictions, disagreements and fighting between them, which in turn made my father distance himself from my mother, to the point that they stopped having intimacy as a couple. They only stayed living in the house together due to the responsibility they both had as parents, to continue raising their youngest children. Besides, uncle Trino also said that my parents' constant fights and arguing made my father a sad, solitary, and unhappy individual, which in turn made him to start drinking and smoking cigarettes every day. Besides, uncle Trino believed and every time my father he had an opportunity, he stayed away from the house to avoid fighting with my mother and avoid being in the house when my mother was practicing and executing acts and events of witchcraft, sorcery, and spiritualism. My father's excesses with the use of alcohol and cigarettes for so many years caused his belly to swell, he could hardly breathe. Hence, we brought him to the hospital, where he stayed for several weeks and was diagnosed by the doctors as having his livers and lungs destroyed due to the use of alcohol and cigarettes. Although the doctors tried to save his life, it was nothing they could do; the harm was already done; my father died in that hospital at a young age of sixty.

Years later after the my father's death and as an adult, I reflected and analyzed his life and based on the story told by my uncle Trino, regarding the type of relationship my parents had; based on my own observations as a child of my father's conduct and behaviors; based in the knowledge I acquired with the study of the Bible; and based on my own experiences and observations of the occult, and how Satan and his demons operate to confuse and to deceive people, I concluded that my father was not only a victim of Satan and those same demons that always chased and lived with my mother but also these same demons pushed my father to fall into the bad habits of drinking alcohol and smoking cigarettes that cost him his life at such an early age. My father lived and shared his life with my mother for more that forty years until his death, and even if he was never aware, he also lived and shared his life with Satan and those same demons that chased and tormented my mother her entire life. Although my father never believed in the occult and never participated directly in any acts or rites of witchcraft, sorcery, or spiritualism, that did not shield him from Satan's attacks and possessions and his demons that always lived with my mother. But even worse, my father never repented from his sins, nor did he ever surrendered his life to Christ. Consequently, my father could not avoid being chased and tormented by Satan and his demons, as they did to my mother, even when he did not want this to happen to him or even when he was never aware of it. 1Peter 5:8,9 "Be sober-minded; be watchful. Your adversary the devil prowls around like a roaring lion, seeking someone to devour. Resist him, firm in your faith, knowing that the same kinds of suffering are being experienced by your brotherhood throughout the world."

Horrific Encounter in a Dark Forest

The practice of the occult and the scary and horror stories that were told almost daily by some people in the community developed in many of us a deep and profound fear of the nights and of dark places. Every time we heard an unfamiliar noise or any strange sound of a bird or an animal, we instinctively associated them with something malign and supernatural. One night when I was about twelve or thirteen years old, one of my oldest brothers invited me to go fishing with him at the nearby Caribbean coast, but since in order to reach that coast, we had to walk five or six miles, by passing through a wide, long and dark forest full of thickets, we prepared two gas burners to light up the road and left the house at around nine o'clock at night, since we had the idea of fishing through the night until the next morning, because according to our estimation, these were the best and most productive hours to fish. Once we reached a wire fence that enclosed and separated the forest from the road, we lighted up one of the gas burner, crossed the wire fence, got into the forest and started walking toward the coast. After walking through that dark forest for a while, we finally arrived at the coast with no problem and started fishing, but after long hours of casting the hooks with the baits, the fish were not biting the hooks with baits, and I got tired and bored of sitting on those hard, craggy and sharp rocks. Thus, I suggested to my brother to stop fishing and to go back home, but since he refused to leave, I decided to leave the coast alone, I grabbed one of the gas burner to light my way up and I walked toward the dark forest that I had to cross to get to the road which would lead me back home. Once in the dark forest, I lighted up the gas burner and started walking, but after I walked at about one hundred meters, I started hearing a noise coming from those dense and dark bushes and trees standing in one side of the road. Somewhat worried and concerned, I directed the gas burner's light toward the direction from where I thought the noise was coming from. Since I did not see anything, I started walking fast, but as I was walking and moving along, suddenly, I also started hearing some squeals coming from the thickets still hear the some squeals coming from the thickets, but in addition to this I also started hearing a screech. Nervous and scared I started walking as fast as I could, trying to distance myself from that place, but as I walked and moved, I could also sense that whatever was making those sound, noise and squeals was also moving at the same speed I was moving. Desperate, I started running at full speed with the gas burner hand lighting up road up, but as I was running, I could also feel that the sound, noise, squeals and screech of the thing that were chasing me was still moving and running at the same speed I was running. Horrified, I kept on running like crazy, and at this point, I was convinced that I was being chased by a malign being such as witch, a Baca, or a demon that was looking to harm me. While I was thinking this, I kept on running at full speed for almost an hour and finally, sweaty and tired, I managed to reach the wire fence that separated the forest from the roadway that would lead me to my house, and it was not after I crossed that fence the noise, sound, squeals and screech of whatever was chasing me stopped.

Once in the roadway, relieved and calmed, I started walking toward my house, and while I was walking in that road, I saw a security guard man who was in the area. I approached him and told him what had happened to me in that forest, but to my surprise, that man in a mocking tone started laughing out loud. I was so ashamed and upset with his attitude that I asked him: Why are you laughing and making a joke of something so serious and horrifying that happened to me? After I said that, the man stopped laughing and with a friendly smile and with a serious look on the face, he told me: "Look, young man, I am not trying to mock you or to laugh at what you told me. What happened is that what you thought was chasing you was not a witch nor a demon or a Baca, it was an owl, and this owl was not chasing you, it was simply following the light that was coming out of the gas burner you was carrying, the fact that owls do not have good vision at night, they instinctively react and follow the movement of light glows or lights reflected in the dark." True or not, the explanation given to me by the security guard really calmed me down because I was convinced that what was chasing me in that dark and scary forest was a demoniac and supernatural being that wanted to harm me. Psalm 32:7 "You are a hiding place for me; you preserve me from trouble; you surround me with shouts of deliverance."

Occultism, Other People

In the community where I lived with my family, a woman called India lived alone in a corner of one of the town's streets. She was a mysterious, strange, and quiet woman who did not have friends, and nobody visited her in her house. Her house's backyard looked like a fortress surrounded with barbwire and covered and protected with dense, thick, and tall trees that prevented the house and the interior of the backyard from being seen from the street, and nobody was ever allowed to enter the backyard without her consent. Many people in the community, including some of her neighbors, believed that India was a witch and that she was seen flying in a broom at night around the neighborhood, looking for new born children to suck their blood and to extract all of their greasy fluids out of their bodies to do witchcraft. Although some people in the community believed that India was indeed a witch, some others did not believed such story. However, there was a time in the community when new born children mysteriously started to die and disappear without an apparent reason or cause for their deaths, and the children who disappeared were never found. Although there was not evidence or proof to accuse India for these children' deaths and disappearances, these events convinced everybody in the community that India was indeed a witch and that she was responsible for the deaths and disappearances of all the community children. One day, a group of people from the community gathered together and went to the police station and reported what was going on in the community with children and formally accused India of being the person responsible for those children deaths and disappearances, but since they could not provide any concrete proof to support their statement, the police dismissed their accusation and did not bother to investigate their complaint. But one day, one of India's neighbor woke up early in the morning, and he noticed a strong odor that was coming from India's house, alarmed he informed other neighbors of such odor and they gathered outside India's backyard shouting her name loudly, but India never responded. Thus, they went to the police station and told them what was happening; this time, the police reacted and sent two agents to India's house to investigate. Once the two agents approached the gate of the backyard, they shouted India's name several times. And since India did not respond, the two agents broke the gate of the backyard and went to the main door of the house, followed by some of India's neighbors. Once again, they started calling her name loudly, and since India neither responded, they broke down the door. But at soon as the door came down and the agents were about to enter the house, the odor coming from the house was so strong that they had to move back and get some piece of rags to cover their mouths and noses to be able to get inside the house. Once inside the house the two agents walked into India's main room and found her corpse badly discomposed lying down in her bed. Then, they walked into a very tiny and discreet room where they found few glass containers and glass jars filled with oily and greasy liquid substances. These findings immediately draw India's neighbors' attention, who claimed that those oily and greasy substances found on those glass jars and containers came from the bodies of those children who had died and disappeared in the community. The news of these findings and the accusation made by these neighbors spread right away throughout the community, and some angry and furious people tried to burn the house with the discomposed corpse of India in it. They had to be stopped by the police to prevent them from doing so.

It had already been more than fifty years since this event occurred. Although nobody was ever able to prove that India was a witch or that those oily and greasy liquids found at her house in those containers and glass jars came from those children who had died and who had disappeared in the community at that time, people in this community still believed this story of India to be true. And even as of today, this tale is still being told in the community and continued to be passed on from generation to generation.

In the community also lived a lady named Prieta, a mentally disturbed person who always had a sad and blank stare look in her face. Although Prieta had family and a place to stay, she was always wandering around in the streets, walking barefoot, smelly, and wearing ragged and dirty clothes. Prieta also used to sit down every day in a low concrete wall located in one of the town's principal streets, spitting and gathering huge puddles of saliva in the floor. She also showed wild and strange behaviors. After just sitting down in that concrete wall, Prieta abruptly and unexpectedly would get up very quickly and would start walking very fast, then she suddenly would stop, then she would start walking very slow, moving her head side to side, then she would take a couple steps back and looked around, as if she was afraid of something, or as if someone was chasing her. Prieta also gestured with her hands, as if she was talking and fighting with some imaginary being by repeating these same words over and over again: "I told you to leave me alone, no, no, no." Then, she would walk very fast and would walk back to the concrete wall where she was sitting just seconds ago and sat down again, spitting saliva all over the place, talking and gesturing, walking back and forward, stopping, fighting, sitting in the same place, getting up and repeating the same words and the same actions and behaviors over and over again for hours.

Some of the older People who knew Prieta since she was a child said that the reason for her mental illness was due to the fact that she worshiped Satan and his demons for many years with the practice of witchcraft, sorcery, and spiritualism and although she stopped this practice many years before, the demons never left her and always chased her up to the point of driving her crazy. One afternoon, a lady who lived in the community was walking by the concrete wall where Prieta always sat down and noticed that Prieta was quiet and not moving, as if she was sleeping or resting under a tree that was next to the concrete wall where Prieta always sat down. The lady, out of curiosity, got close to Prieta and shouted her name, but since Prieta did not move and did not respond, the lady then touched her gently in her shoulder, and Prieta's body slowly started to slide to the side and fell on top of those puddles of saliva that she herself gathered in the floor of that street. Prieta was dead. What sad life that of Prieta! Although she had a family, she died alone in the street, chased by Satan and his demons whom she worshiped for many years.

The Bright Star of the Family

William, the eldest of my brothers was a noble, calm, and composed temper man. Nothing ever bothered or altered William's mood, behavior, or demeanors, who was always ready and available to listen, advise, and help anybody with any problem he or she may have had. When William was a teenager, he suffered and accident while riding a wagon pulled by horses, he lost his body balance falling to the floor in the street, and one of his legs fell under one of the wagon's wheels, breaking and crushing it up to his knee and had to be amputated. After this accident, William surrendered his life to Christ jointed a Christian Pentecostal church. Years later, he became a missionary pastor of that church, traveling and moving around from place to place, throughout the entire country of the Dominican Republic, building and establishing churches. As a result of his accident and the lost of half of his leg, William had an artificial leg and a cane to be able to walk. Thus, every time that William walked, he limped and bent his body to the side where he had the artificial leg. Besides, he always carried an old black and big bag full of his books and clothes, which were his only and all material possession he had because they were giving to him by his brothers and sisters of the churches he visited. It was very common to find William standing in a corner of any street during the day, sweaty and tired, resting and taking a break, due to his physical limitation, the huge effort he had to make when he walked, and due to his way of dressing with ties, suit and long shirts under the blazing sun of the Caribbean. But in spite of his physical limitation and despite being so poor, William was a very happy man; he lived his life as someone who had everything he needed; my brother never complained or lamented, and his attitudes and behaviors made me reflect on the words of the Apostle Paul who say in Philippians 4:11-12 "I am not saying this because I am in need, for I have learned to be content whatever the circumstances. I know what it is to be in need, and I know what it is to have plenty. I have learned the secret of being content in any and every situation, whether well fed or hungry, whether living in plenty or in want."

I remember that we (the family) had to wait months and sometimes years for William to visit us because the nature of his ministry as missionary pastor required from him to travel a lot and to move from place to place, building and establishing churches, which prevented him from visiting us as frequently as he wanted to. However, when he did come to visit us at the house where I lived with my family, I was very happy to see him and to feel his presence in the house because during the whole time he stayed with us, he prayed days and nights, he preached the gospel, and sang a lot of Christian songs all the times. He also used to conduct Christian worship services and prayers all over the places in the community where we lived, in houses, in the backyards and in any streets. William's spiritual and holy presence in our house was so powerful that during the whole time he stayed with us, all form and manifestation of witchcraft, sorcery, and spiritualism practiced by my mother and sisters stopped, and the mood and environment in the house was positive, peaceful and tranquil. I really enjoyed having William around in the house because having him around, I felt safe and protected emotionally and spiritually, and I could also rest and sleep better. William was truly a man of God, a good, humble, and special human being who spent most of his life dedicated to serve God and humanity. My brother was so committed to God and his ministry that he got married for the first time at an advanced age of fifty-five, and he had his first and only daughter when he was fifty six. William was indeed the light and the spiritual leader of our family, a man of faith whose conduct and behaviors represented the highest moral, human, and Christian values, not only for my family but to the human race and to God. I do not think that I exaggerate when I say that William was an angel sent by God to our family and to the world to illuminate us and to show us the right spiritual path. "Because when there was darkness, he brought light; When there was defenselessness; he brought protection; and where there was fear; he brought tranquility and faith." William died almost ten years ago due to a prostate cancer at the age of eighty, but there is not doubt in my mind that the Most high God will reward him for his work in the resurrection of the righteous. May God be praised! John 11:25-26 "I am the resurrection and the life. The one who believes in me will live, even though they die; and whoever lives by believing in me will never die. Do you believe this?"

The Effects of Occultism and Personal Growth (the author)

The practices and the horrifying and diabolic acts of witchcraft, sorcery, and spiritualism that I witnessed and lived alongside my family from my childhood through my adolescent years not only caused me serious psychological, emotional, and spiritual traumas and conflicts but it also affected the relationship I had with those members of my family, including my mother, who practiced it. I was so ashamed and guilty for the practice of the occult by those family's members that I never talked about it to anybody outside of my family, and it was until more than fifty years later, after the occurrences of these events, that I dared to write and publish this book, in order to reveal to the world, the horrifying experiences that I lived and suffered during that period of my life. I remember occasions being in the house along with my mother and my sisters and when I sensed or suspected that any of them was going to be possessed by demons, or when any of them was going to engage in any diabolic act of occultism, I would always walk out of the house, and I would not come back to it until I was sure that whatever act of occultism they were executing had ended. I also would avoid sleeping alone in the same room at night with my mother or my sisters because I was afraid to walk up in the middle of the night to witness a diabolic possession or any other acts of occultism executed by any of them. Similarly, I would avoid being with my mother or any of my sisters alone in a solitary place at any time during the day or night because any time I was in an isolated place with any of them, I always had a feeling that something diabolic was going to happen in my presence. This, in turn, made me bring back to life those horrifying, traumatic, and disturbing memories and feelings I lived alongside them since I was child to my adolescent years. I also behaved the same way when I was listening the radio or watching television; if I heard or saw someone commenting and talking about any subject related to the occult, I would reject and condemn that action, and I would immediately turn off the radio or the television. The same thing happened when I was reading a book or a magazine; if there was any mention of the occult, I would close that book or magazine, and I would not read them ever. In a like manner, I reacted when I was in the theater watching a movie, any time I saw a scene of witchcraft, sorcery or spiritualism, I would walk out of that theater and I would never see that movie again nor I would ever recommend it to anyone.

The psychological, emotional, and spiritual conflicts and traumas I suffered from my childhood to my adolescent years, as a result of the practices of the occult carried out by family's members and other people in my presence, worsened even further because, in the meantime, I was also going through the process and formation of my own personal identity and personality, dealing with all of those physical, hormonal, psychological and emotional changes typical of the adolescence, and I had to face and resolve them on my own, without getting any help or guidance from anyone. During that time, I was very depressed, I isolated myself from other people, and I spent a lot of time, alone, quiet and thoughtful, and although I always attended school every day and I passed all of my exams and courses, I had to make a great effort to be able to accomplish it. I also lived in a state of awful confusion, filled with mixed feelings, conflicting emotions, doubts and insecurities about myself. I always asked to myself the following questions: Who am I? Who am I going to be when I grow up? What my future and my family future be? But since I could not find concrete and real answers to these questions, I sometimes, started writing in the air with my finger, in an imaginary way, my own answers to my own questions. Some of the people who at that time saw me writing in the air thought that I was losing my mind or that I was crazy; however, doing those mental exercises of writing in the air served as a therapy for me because in some way and some how helped me to ease and to relieve all of those disturbing and conflicting feelings and emotions that I was carrying with me during that stage of my life. Another thing that also helped me to overcome my psychological, emotional and spiritual traumas and conflicts at that time was the fact that I was a good reader. I spent a lot of time reading about every thing that fell in my hands; I used to read the Bible, books, magazines, newspapers, short stories, and other literatures. I also enjoyed singing, dancing and listening to music. Since all of these activities required dedication and concentration, I submerged and took refuge in these hobbies and pastimes and this, in turn, allowed me to forget and to escape, at least for a moment, from all of the traumas and conflicts I was facing at that time of my life.

Living close to the Caribbean coasts, beaches and forest of the Dominican Republic was another thing that contributed to my personal growth and to overcome my psychological, emotional and spiritual state of mind. Since I had free access to those places, I spent whole nights on those coasts facing the sea, fishing, meditating, talking and thinking to myself aloud, imagining a better future for me and my family, relaxing and looking at the sky full of bright stars and its moon at night. Similarly, I spent entire days in those beautiful and wide beaches swimming, lying down in the white sands, walking in the shores of the beaches, smelling and breathing the clean air and the cool breeze that came from the sea and from those beaches. And looking at the blue sky and the water with white foams in the beaches that for a moment seemed to look blue and other time seemed to be green. Likewise, I spent entire days in the forest hunting wild animals, listening to the sounds and songs of birds, looking and observing the different colors and shades of the trees and flowers, gathering and eating fruits and vegetables which grew freely and wildly in the forest, and enjoying the peace and tranquility offered by the forest. Furthermore, I practiced different sports, I played baseball, boxing , and swimming. And the execution of all those physical and mental activities and the direct physical contact that I had with nature served me as therapy and helped me to overcome all of the conflicts and psychological problems I had in my adolescence. These activities also helped me control my emotional and spiritual state, mold and smooth my temperament and character, and train and develop my own personality and identity.

One other thing that contributed to my personal growth, although it may be contradictory, was that during my childhood and my adolescence, I lived and observed all those demoniac rites and acts of witchcraft, sorcery, and spiritualism executed by some members of my family. Because these experiences allowed me to have a better understanding of how Satan and his demons operate, the strategies and tactics they use to cheat and catch their victims, and how they harm those people who worship them. Also, by having these experiences, I learned how to recognize, distinguish and differentiate when things come from Satan or from God, to be able to defend and protect myself against the attacks of Satan and his demons, and to warn other people so that they can also defend and protect themselves against the attacks of the maligns, and to avoid falling into their traps. The writing of this book was another thing that contributed in a big way to my personal growth and to be able to overcome my psychological, emotional and spiritual state of mind because during the process of writing it, I had to bring to life, confront and cast out all of those experiences and traumatic memories which were buried very deep in my mind and in my soul for more than fifty years. This book's writing also allowed me to close once for all that stormy period of my live and helped me to get rid of that family secret as well as that feeling of shame and guilt that I always dragged and carried with me for so many years. My higher education and my professional backgrounds also played a huge role in my personal growth and in overcoming my psychological, emotional and spiritual conflicts and problems. Because, as a professional sociologist, I had the opportunity to read and to study people's social, emotional, psychological, and mental processes and behaviors. This, in turn, allowed me to use and apply this acquired knowledge to understand and recognize my own conflicts and problems, and how to deal with them.

However, the keys to my personal growth and to overcome my psychological, emotional, and spiritual problems, without a doubt, were the following: the study and scrutinize of the Bible, listening and seeing the preaching of Christian pastors and evangelists in social medias, radios, televisions, and the prayers I always receive from members of my family and friends. Although I have never been a dogmatic or a religious individual who attend churches regularly, I do believe in Jesus Christ and I do have a personal and direct relationship and communication with God every day of my life. For the honor and glory of Him! Ephesians 6:10-18 "Finally, be strong in the Lord and in the strength of his might. Put on the whole armor of God, that you may be able to stand against schemes of the evil. For we do nor wrestle against flesh and blood, but against the rulers, against the authorities, against the cosmic powers over this present darkness, against the spiritual forces of evil in the heavenly places. Therefore take up the whole armor of God, that you may be able to withstand in the evil day, and having done all, to stand firm. Stand therefore, having fastened on the belt of truth, and having put on the breastplate of righteousness, and, as shoes for your feet, having put on the readiness given by the gospel of peace. In all circumstances take up the shield of faith, with which you can extinguish all the flaming darts of the evil one, and take the helmet of salvation, and the sword of the Spirit, which is the word of God, praying at all times in the Spirit, with all prayer and supplication. To that end, keep alert with all perseverance, making supplication for all the saints. Amen!"

Conclusion

The real stories, anecdotes, and acts of witchcrafts, sorceries, and spiritualisms told in this book. The harms and traumas that these diabolic experiences caused to those people who directly or indirectly participated in those events need to be known to the world so that people can understand that nothing good or positive can ever be achieved with the practice of the occultism. These experiences can also serve as a warning for those people who are at this moment practicing the occult for them to realize that the same thing that happened to me, to some members of my family, and to other people in the community can also happened to them and their family if they do not stop worshiping Satan and his demons, repent of their sins and surrender their lives to Christ, before it is too late. Likewise, these experiences can be used to educate and to send a message to those people who do not know of the existence of Satan and his demons and to those who believed that Satan is a game, an invention or an imagination, for them to learn that these supernatural beings and entities are real. They have the power to deceive, confuse, separate and destroy those who worship them as well as their entire family for generations. Similarly, these real experiences can be utilized to teach people of the strategies and tricks that Satan and his demons use to attract, catch and make people fall in their traps to avoid being the victims of these maligns. Finally, these real stories, experiences, and anecdotes of witchcrafts, sorceries, and spiritualisms can be utilized to send a message to all of those people who worship Satan and his demons with the practice of the occult, for them to understand that by doing this, they are not only signing a pact of spiritual death with these maligns but they are also inviting them to enter to their lives, to their house and to control and harm their own life, as well as the lives of all members of their family who live with them. Even worst, with the occult practice, they are also offending God, and at the same time they are separating themselves from all of his graces, from all of his mercies, and from all of his glories. Amen! Leviticus 20:6 "I will set my face against anyone who turns to mediums and spiritists to prostitute themselves by following them, and I will cut them off from their people."

Author's Personal Comments About the Book

Writing this, my first book, was a very difficult and distressing task for me, not only because of the strict discipline and the great physical and mental effort that required the solitary and sometimes overwhelming act of having to seat down and write hours after hours and days after days for almost four years but also because during the process of writing it, I had to face and bring to life all of those disturbing and traumatic memories, images, scenes and acts of witchcraft, sorceries and spiritualisms that I lived and witnessed with my family during my childhood and my adolescent years, which left on me indelible footprints. Having to mention in this book the participation of some members of my family in those horrendous, diabolic, and shameful acts, and having to reveal this family's well-kept secret of the occult that I held with me for more than fifty years was also a very difficult thing for me to do because it touched very intimate and sensible fibers of my live and the lives of some members of my family. Furthermore, during the process of writing this book, I had great doubts, hesitations, and fears because bringing back to mind those demoniac memories and images of those terrifying and traumatic events of the occult, I felt that I was exposing myself to call and to attract Satan and his demons to my life, to my house and my family. Consequently, there were times when I had to stop writing, to read the Bible, pray and ask God for spiritual protection to continue with the writing of this book. Similarly, I had to look for advices and spiritual guidance from José Matamoros, a Christian pastor and friend of mine who provided me valuable spiritual advices and guidance. He also read the first draft of my book and made some suggestions and recommendations that were helpful for me to continue writing this book.

Finding and interviewing members of my family to get their consents and write this book was also very difficult for me to do because after more than fifty years of the occurrences of those events, most members of my family had already died, and those who are still alive, some of them reside in the United States where I live, and other are still residing in the Dominican Republic. Thus, I interviewed first the ones who reside in the United States and later I had to travel several times to the Dominican Republic to interview the ones who reside there. However, during the interviews I had with all family members, some of them were opposed to the idea of me writing this book, claiming that the practice of occultism in our family was a well- kept secret. They also felt that revealing this secret in this book was a treason to the memories of those members of my family who have died and a shame for those of us who are still alive. Nonetheless, after I explained to them that revealing this secret in the book was precisely what all of us needed to get rid of and to free ourselves from all of those disturbing memories and feeling of guilt and shame that we all had been carrying around for so many years, they all agreed and granted me their consents to write this book with the conditions of not using the real name of any members of my family who are either dead or alive. I agreed and accepted their conditions, but I emphasized to them that under no circumstance I would change or alter my memories and recollections of the events as they occurred or the way I felt, and I lived them under no circumstance. At the end, we all in the family agreed and here is the book, hoping that it can be of some help for anybody who reads it.

Glosary

Bacá: A malignant spirit that goes around and protects the belongings of its owner under the appearance of an animal.

Deity: A supernatural being considered divine or sacred

Divinity: The state of things that are believed to come from a supernatural power

Enchantment: The state of being under a spell produced by magic.

Exorcism: The expulsion or attempted expulsion of a supposed evil spirit from a person or place.

Healer: A person or thing that heals.

Hex: A curse or malicious wish.

Incantation: A written or recited formula of words designed to produce a particular effect and by using natural an medicinal plants and herbs.

Magic: The use of means such as charms or spells believed to have supernatural power over natural forces.

Malign: Evil in nature or effect; malevolent.

Medium: Uses his or her psychic or intuitive abilities to see the past, present and future events of a person by turning into the spirit energy surrounding that person.

Occult: Supernatural, mystical, or magical beliefs, practices, or phenomena paranormal.

Occultism: Various theories and practices involving a belief in and knowledge or use of supernatural or supernormal powers.

Omen: An event regarded as a portent of good or evil.

Possession: The state of having, owning, or controlling something.

Potion: A liquid with healing or magical properties.

Quack: A person who falsely pretends to have medical skills or knowledge.

Santera/Santero: A person excessively devoted to saints

Shaman: A person regarded as having to, and influence in the world of good and evil spirits.

Sorcerer: A person who claims or is believed to have magic powers.

Sorcery: The use of power gained from the assistance or control of evil spirits.

Sortilege: A method of divination through the casting of lots.

Spell: A spoken word or forms of words held to have magic power.

Spiritualism: A belief that the spirits of the dead exist and have both the ability and the inclination to communicate with the living.

Trance: A half-conscious state of mind characterized by an absence of response to external stimuli.

Wake: Hold a vigil beside (someone who has died).

Witch: A woman thought to have magic powers

Witchcraft: The practice of black magic.

Wizard: A man who claims or is believed to have magic powers (a wizard)

Worship: The feeling or expression of reverence and adoration for a deity.

www.ingramcontent.com/pod-product-compliance
Lightning Source LLC
LaVergne TN
LVHW091605060526
838200LV00036B/998